10 Scarves and Cowls

to knit and crochet

Sharon Bates

DEDICATION

To "Yarnies" everywhere

CONTENTS

INTRODUCTION

This book contains
patterns to knit and crochet.

1

SHIBORI MOBIUS
(KNITTING)

Webster's Dictionary -
Definition of MÖBIUS "STRIP"
: a one-sided surface that is constructed from a long rectangle by holding one end fixed, rotating the opposite end through 180 degrees, and joining it to the first end. The

definition of this Mobius is a never ending one sided surface. See the link to Cat Borhdi's great video on you tube.

https://www.youtube.com/watch?v=LVnTda7F2V4

Materials: Queensland Collection – Uluru or any non-wool sport/fingering weight yarn. 250 yds or more.
NORO Cyochin – or any aran/bulky 100% wool yarn. (Less than 100 yds.) Wool)

Needles: US 10.5 - 40"+ needle
Stitches used: garter, Yarn over Knit, Mobius Cast on

Before starting; if you have not done the Cat Bhordi's Mobius cast on then go to you tube at: https://www.youtube.com/watch?v=LVnTda7F2V4

With Cyochin (wool) Cast on 120 stitches and place marker, join and knit the first round until you slip the marker from needle to needle.
The first knit row is the hardest row – Don't throw in the towel just yet! Tension here is not important; just muddle your way through…. Also, don't worry about which leg you knit into, the cast on stitches will be coming off the needle back and forth.

Change to Uluru yarn and
Row 1: *K2 tog, YO* to marker. (slipping marker as before)
Row 2: Purl to marker. Repeat these two rows 10 more times.

Change to Cyochin; knit to marker, purl to marker.

Change to Uluru yarn and *K 2 tog, YO* to marker.

Purl to marker. Repeat these two rows10 more times.

Change to Cyochin; knit to marker, purl to marker. Bind off loosely.

Wash the cowl in your washer with a towel or other heavy object on **Hot/Cold** cycle.
When done, check to see that the wool is felted. If not, then repeat.
Dry with a fan.

2

TAIYO MOBIUS
(KNITTING)

Materials:
1 skein NORO Taiyo in your color choice.

Needles: US 11, 40"

Cast on 108 (144) stitches in the "Magic Mobius cast on" including the slip loop.

If you have not done the mobius cast on previously; see the link to Cat Borhdi's great video on you tube. **https://www.youtube.com/watch?v=LVnTda7F2V4**

Put a marker onto the right needle and Knit the first round as in the video. *The marker will be on the cable, not the needle.* Because it is on the cable it is half way around your Mobius as you are knitting both sides in succession.

Continue knitting until the marker slips from needle point to needle point. This completes a **full** round. Each full round actually knits both edges (one continuous Mobius edge)

Pattern Stitch:
Feather and Fan (12 stitch repeat)
Row 1: Knit
Row 2: Purl
Row 3: *K2 tog, K2 tog, YO, K1, YO, K1, YO K1, YO, K1, K2 tog, K2 tog.* 9 (12) times placing markers between sets.
Row 4: Knit

After casting on and completing the first knit round, continue in the Feather and Fan Lace stitch pattern. 8x (6x)

Bind off loosely.

The Mobius scarf has become a staple in our wardrobes for those chilly air conditioned places even during hot weather. They are a fashion statement and an adornment for a plain outfit or a face in need of color nearby. What better to dress up jeans and a tee shirt than a light and airy cowl? This Mobius is for those cooler weather days, as it is knit with Taiyo, an aran weight yarn. It is cotton, silk and wool and it is colorful, the sheer visual weight of it lends itself to an outer garment but it is soft against the skin. It is knit in the feather and fan lace pattern to trap air and insulate with lots of color and less bulk.

I have included the cast on information that is on You Tube as it is the easiest way to help you understand the Mobius cast on and get you started knitting with your 40" circular knitting needles.

3

COWL IN
LACE MERINO
(CROCHET)

This cowl is worked in the round.

Materials: Ella Rae Lace Merino fingering. One skein tonal and one skein multi colored.

Needles: size "F" aluminum hook or '"D" Palmwood crochet hook.

Stitches used: Chain (Ch), Half Double Crochet (HDC), Double Crochet (DC), slip stitch (Sl)

Making a decrease in Double Crochet:

Work the first half on a DC in the next stitch, work another first half in the next stitch, and then work both second halves together to create a 1 stitch decrease.

Cowl:
In color A: Ch 164. Join
Ch 2, DC in 3rd chain, work all around and join at beginning.
Join color B: Ch 1, turn work.
HDC all around, join at beginning.

With color A: Ch 2, turn work, DC all around, join at beginning. Cut color A yarn and work in.

With color B: Ch 4, *DC in 2nd stitch, Ch 1* join at beginning,
Ch 4, *DC in 2nd stitch, Ch 1* join at beginning.

Join color A: Ch 2, turn work, DC around, Join. Ch 2, turn, *DC 5, work one decrease,* finish with DC's to end, join at beginning.

With color B: Ch 1, HDC all around, join cut and weave in end

With Color A: join and *ch 5. In 4th stitch from join, make a Sl stitch.* these should come out fairly even. But if not fudge the last connection.
Row 2, sl st 2x to get to 3rd stitch in chain. *Ch 5, join in 3rd ch on next loop*.
Row 3: repeat row 2.

With color B: join at 3rd ch on loop, *Ch 3, Sl 1 at 3rd ch on loop* join at end.
In same direction, Ch 2, HDC to end, join.

With color a: join, turn, DC around, join. Cut color A and work in.

With color B: Ch 4, *DC in 2nd stitch, Ch 1* join at beginning,
Ch 4, *DC in 2nd stitch, Ch 1* join at beginning.

Join color A: Ch 2, turn work, DC around, Join. Ch 2, turn, *DC 5, work one decrease,*,
finish with DC's to end, join at beginning.

With color B: Ch 1, turn work.
HDC all around, join at beginning.

With color A: Ch 2, turn work, DC all
around, join at beginning.

With color B: Ch 1, turn work.
HDC all around, join at beginning.

With Color A: join and Ch 5. In 4th stitch
from join, make a Sl stitch.* these should
come out fairly even. But if not fudge the
last connection.
Row 2, Sl st 2x to travel the chain to the 3rd
stitch in chain. *Ch 5, join in 3rd ch on next
loop*.
Row 3: repeat row 2.

With color B: join at 3rd ch on loop, *Ch 3, Sl 1 at 3rd ch on loop* join at end.
In same direction, Ch 2, HDC to end, join.
With color A: Ch 2, turn work, DC all around, join at beginning.
Ch 2, turn, DC around, join at end. Cut weave in all ends.

4

FOREST FIRE SCARF
(CROCHET)

Materials: One skein Ella Rae Superwash Lace Merino in Red/ green fingering and one skein in green /grey tonals.
Size "J" crochet hook.

Stitches used:
Chain, Slip stitch, Single crochet, Double Crochet, Treble Crochet, Double treble crochet
Definition of a post: The stitch in the row below. Stitch into the top opening of the stitch below.

A chain 2 represents the first stitch in the new row.

Chain 4, DC in 2nd ch from hook, DC, turn. (two stitches made)
Increase on one side: (every other row)
Ch 2, DC in 2nd ch from hook (increase 1), Dc to end (make sure you dc over the ch in the last row to keep edge even). Turn Ch 2, Dc in next stitch (not chain bottom, but first open post), DC in chain post. (3 stitches)

Place marker: Place marker at this side of your work and move up the ide as your work progresses. This is your reminder to increase at this edge only.

Increase the same way every other (marked) row until you get to 40 (60) rows. Place another marker at tip of increases.

Decreases:
Ch 2, Dc in first open post, DC to end including last ch post. Turn, Ch2, Dc in every open post NOT including the last chain post. (decrease 1). Bind off at last two stitches, work in the ends.

Connect Green yarn at same end and working over the increase side first. Ch 1, Sc around making a sc 3 times in two rows. (one in first DC side, one at the post opening and one in the side of the second DC) repeat until you have reached the start.

Chain 4, *Trc in the second open post below (skip one), Ch 1* to tip. Ch 1, Trc in tip stitch. * Ch1, Trc in second stitch*, to end (top of ch post below)

DC in post of first Trc 5 times to create a shell, sl st into the top of the 2rd Trc. (shell created) *DC in top of next Trc post 5 times, sl st in next Trc post* to just before the middle ch.

Tip: Ch 5, Sl st in next post.

Decrease side: *DC in next post 5 times, sl st in next post* to end.
Turn.
Last row: Ch 3 from the start of the first shell, *DC in the middle of the 5 DC's of the shell, Ch 2, Dc in same middle stitch, Ch 1* to last shell on this side of center, Trc in center 5 chains, Ch1, DTrc, Ch1, Trc, Ch 1. *DC in middle stitch of the 5 stitch shell, Ch2, DC in same stitch, Ch1*. Repeat to end, DC in top of last Trc. Finish. Weave ends.

Wet Block, pin along the straight edge first, then stretch and pin at the spaces between double crochets, middle and end tips. Dry with a fan.

5

LACE SCARF
(KNITTING)

Material:
Araucania Ruca Multi (sport) or any yarn you fancy, really!
US size 6, if you use anything bigger than sport weight; go up in needle size to your liking.

Gage: 6/ in

Stitch pattern: (4 st repeat)+2 selv.
Row 1: K1 selv. st, *K2, yo, Sl 2 knitwise, insert left needle back into slipped stitches, K 2 tog.*, K1 selv.
Row 2: K1 selv, *P2, yo, P 2 tog*, K1 selv.

Scarf:

Cast on 34 sts. K 6 rows in garter ending
on the WS.
Knit in pattern st. 4 repeats. (8 rows) ending
on the WS.
Knit 4 rows in garter st.
Knit in pattern st 8 repeats, (16 rows) ending
on the WS.
Knit 4 rows in garter st.
Continue until you reach desired
scarf length.
(60 inches average) bind off and
work in ends.

6

STRATTA SCARF
(CROCHET)

Materials: One Ball Zauberball Crazy *or* Stash accumulation of sock yarn leftovers
Hook: US size "H"

Stitches used: Chain, Single Crochet, Half Double Crochet (YO before SC, pull through all three)

Scarf:
Chain Loosely 114 sts, Skip two chains and HDC into the rest of the stitches to the end.
* Turn, Ch1, HDC in Ch 1 stitch base *(Increase 1)* and to 4 sts from the end, SC. *(dec 3)*
Turn, SC 1, HDC to end, HDC again in last post stitch *(Increase 1)*

*Repeat these 2 rows until there are only 2 stitches to crochet. End. Work in threads.
Wet Block to shape desired.
Note: I inserted a row of: Ch 3, *Skip1 st, DC in next st, Ch 1* for one row to add interest.*

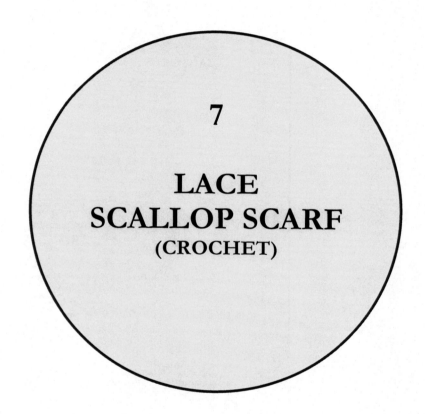

7

**LACE
SCALLOP SCARF**
(CROCHET)

Materials: 1 ball Noro Taiyo Sock, Size "F" crochet hook.

Body: Chain 24, 3 sts from last chain DC1, * Ch 1, DC1 in second chain, (skipping one stitch)* to end (21 stitches)
Turn, Ch3, *Ch 1, DC1 in DC stitch below (second open stitch)* across. Continue for 72 inches, Making sure there is an even number of spaces between "grid lines". Break yarn.

Edging:
At opposite corner from ending (so the yarn color is different)
Start at corner make a slip st.
Using the grid lines as places to make stitches, *DC5 times in first grid line.
Slip stitch in next grid line*. This creates a scallop.
Make scallops in this fashion all around the scarf. End, tie in ends.

8

COLOR PLAY SCARF
(KNITTING)

Materials: Zauberball Crazy by Schoppel colors A: 2092 and B: 2081 one each.

Gauge: 6 stitches per inch

Needles: US size 5

Section 1:
With Color 1:
Cast on 72 stitches,
Row 1: Knit (RS) to last 2 stitches, K2tog.
Row 2: Knit

With color 2:
Row 3: Knit to last 2 stitches, K2tog.
Row 4: Purl
I changed Row 4 every 6th row to a *P1, *YO, P2tog* to create a lace detail.
Repeat until 1 stitch remains.

Section 2:
With Color 1:
On the RS, Pick up 105 sts. All other Row 1's: KFB, Knit to last stitch, KFB
Row 2: On WS Knit
Row 3: With Color 2: KFB, Knit to last stitch, KFB.
Row 4: Purl
Repeat Rows 1 - 4, 11 more times; changing Row 4 to P1, *YO, P2tog* lace pattern on the 10th repeat.
Knit rows 1 and 2 again and then bind off knit-wise on the WS.

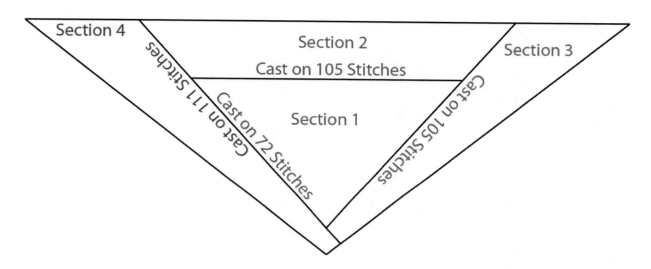

Section 3:

With color 1: On the RS, Pick up 105 sts. All other Row 1's: Knit to last stitch, KFB
Row 2: Knit.
Row 3: With Color 2 - Knit to last stitch KFB
Row 4: First one: P1,*YO, P2tog* lace pattern. All other Row 4's: Purl.
Repeat full rows one time.

SHORT ROWS: (repeat 3 and all other repeats)
Row 1: Use BOTH colors and Knit 6 stitches, drop Color 2 and PM, Knit to last stitch, KFB.
Row 2: Knit to marker, Remove Marker, turn.
Row 3: with BOTH colors, K6, Place Marker, drop color 1 and Knit to last st, KFB.
Row 4: Purl to marker, RM, Turn
Continue until there are less than 6 stitches from the marker to the end of the row.
Cut color 2,
With Color 1: Purl.
Next row: Purl.

Bind off Knit-wise.

Section 4:
On the RS, Pick up 111 sts.
Next row: Row Purl, Next row Purl.
All other Row 1's: KFB, Knit to end.
Row 2: On WS Knit.
Row 3: KFB, Knit to end.
Row 4: Purl.
Row 4: Purl. (Second repeat: P1,*YO, P2tog* lace pattern)

SHORT ROWS: (repeat 3 and all other repeats)
Row 1: KFB, Knit to 6 stitches before end, PM, turn.
Row 2: Knit.
Row 3: KFB, Knit to 6 stitches before marker, PM, turn.
Row 4: Purl.
Repeat until less than 6 stitches remain. Cut Color 2
With Color 1: Knit and remove all markers.
Next row: Knit.
Bind off Knit-wise.

Work in any ends. Wet block.

This is a hat in the Entrelac stitch

The pattern is in the "Just for NORO" book
Or online at www.ravelry.com/designers/sharon-bates

9
ENTRELAC SCARF
(KNITTING)

Materials: Fingering weight, long color-change yarn. I used my handspun singles at Jackson St Fiber Arts.

Size needle to fit yarn (US 3 or 4 suggested)

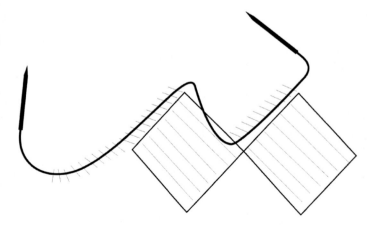

Pattern: Step 1: Cast on 10 sts, knit in

Stockinette for 20 rows ending with a knit row. Step 2: Cast (purl) on 10 sts to the left of your first step, knit in stockinette stitch for 20 rows ending with a knit row.

You now have 2 "squares" next to each other.

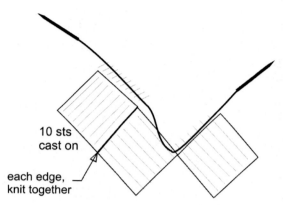

10 sts cast on

each edge, knit together

Step 3: Cast (purl) on 10 sts, purl those sts back to st. 9, purl last st and first loop of 2nd square together. Continue in this pattern until the last loop from the previous square are used up.

You can see the squares are being created on a slant. So this whole row of squares are slanted to the right.

Step 4: Pick up 10 sts on the edge of Step 2 square. Knit back 10 sts being careful not to knit onto square before. Purl back 9 sts, knit 10th st and first loop together and continue like square 3.

Step 5: pick up 10 sts at edge of square 1, continue in st. st. for a total of 20 rows. Ending with a purl row. Bind off those 10 sts and leave the loop as the first stitch of the next step. (Square 6)

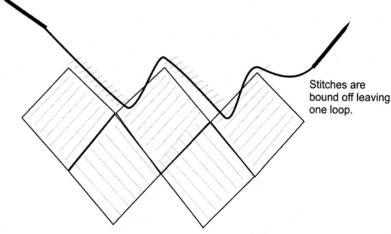

Stitches are bound off leaving one loop.

Step 6: Next row of 2 left slanting squares: Pick up 9 more sts on

..... left edge of the 5th square so you can work the new row of slanting left squares. Continue in customary square knitting, picking up loops at the end of the knit rows. Always ending with a knit row on a left slanting square. (This square is the same as square 1)

Step 7: Continue to pick up your 10 sts and continue the second square for this row. As you may have noticed, the first left slanting row of squares there are 2, then the second row or of right slanting rows, there are 3 squares. This repeats itself for the full length of the scarf.

This step is the same as square 2.

Step 8: repeat from square 3 to the end of the scarf. My suggestion is 5-6 feet long ending in a left slanting 2 square row and binding off after each square is finished.

10
BRICK WARMER
COWL
(KNITTING)

Materials: 2 Classic Superwash, 1 Painted Sky (light worsted or DK)
Needles: US 9 - 32" and US 10.5 - 32"

With Classic Superwash and size 9 needle, Cast on 200 stitches.
Join and Knit in stockinette for 8 rows.
Row 9: Pick up one side of first cast on edge stitch; place it on the left needle, K2tog.
Pick up next side of cast on edge stitch and place it on left needle, K2tog. Continue all 200 stitches creating a rolled edge.
Row 10: Purl
With larger needle;
Row 11, 12, 13: with contrasting color; K2, *Sl1, K3* around, K1.
Row 14: Knit
Row 15: Purl
Row 16, 17, 18: *Sl1, K3* around.

Repeat rows 11- 18 as many times as it takes to finish the contrasting color.
(about 8 times)
With classic Superwash and smaller needle; knit a row and a purl row.
Knit 8 rows stockinette and join to back of work just before garter ditch (as in first rolled edge) as you bind off each stitch. Finish ends.

Wet block and dry beneath a fan.

ABOUT THE AUTHOR

I currently live in Roseburg, Oregon.
I run an online store with my designer knits
and commercial yarns specializing in kits, handspun yarns
and natural fibers. I am also the author of:

A Knitter's Notebook of Yarn Secrets
and
Just for NORO
on Amazon and Kindle

Coming soon
Workshops for the Stash Collector

Thanks for buying this book of patterns.
You can find individual patterns on Amazon and Kindle
by searching for Sharon Bates
or at
www.ravelry.com/designers/sharon-bates

http://www.jacksonstarts.com
Sharon@jacksonstarts.com

Made in the USA
Middletown, DE
03 November 2015